Attack of the Killer Spider

Karl dumped the shopping on the table.

"How come I ended up carrying all the heavy stuff?" he asked Adam.

"Sorry, mate," grinned Adam. "My turn next time."

"I'll believe that when I see it," joked Karl.

"Hey, Karl," asked Adam. "What's black and hairy and bigger than your hand?"

"I don't know," said Karl.

"I don't know either," said Adam, "but it's crawling up your arm."

Karl looked down and saw a huge spider.

"AAARGH!" he cried. "Where did that come from?"

DEADLY!

Contents

Helen Chapman

Story illustrated by Carl Pearce

Heinemann

In this story

 Karl

 Adam

 Karl's mum

 The doctor

Tricky words

- believe
- crawling
- swayed
- double
- breathe
- cinema
- Casualty
- oxygen
- medicine
- wandering

Introduce these tricky words and help the reader when they come across them later!

Story starter

Karl and Adam were best friends. One day, they had been to the market to get some fruit and vegetables for Karl's mum. Karl was carrying a heavy shopping bag.

The spider dropped on to the table.
As Karl tried to flick it off the table,
the spider sank its fangs into his hand.
"Ow!" Karl yelled.
"I'll get it," said Adam, and he picked up
a lunchbox and scooped the spider into it.
"Gotcha!" he said.

"That's the biggest spider I've ever seen," said Adam, and he took a photo of it with his mobile phone.

"I might keep it as a pet," said Karl, "so don't put the lid on too tightly." Suddenly, Karl swayed, then he fell against Adam.

"Are you OK?" asked Adam.

Would you like a spider as a pet?

"I feel really dizzy," said Karl, "and my hand hurts."

"It looks gross!" said Adam. "Do you think you should tell your mum?"

"No," said Karl, "she'll only be in a stress. Let's go or we'll miss that film."

The boys set off. They didn't see the spider crawl out of the box and into Adam's bag.

On the bus Karl said to Adam, "I feel really odd."

"You *look* really odd," said Adam.

Then Karl bent double. "I can't breathe," he said. "My chest really hurts."

"Look, mate," said Adam, "I think we had better go to the hospital, not the cinema."

At Casualty, the doctor made Karl lie down.

"What hurts?" she asked.

"My chest feels like it's going to burst," said Karl.

"And he went all dizzy on the bus," said Adam.

The doctor set up an oxygen mask to help Karl breathe.

Then the doctor saw Karl's hand.

"What happened?" she asked.

"A spider bit him," said Adam.

"A spider?" said the doctor. "What sort of spider?"

"I don't know," said Adam, "but I've got a photo of it."

"Good," said the doctor. "I'll send it to the zoo. Someone there will know what sort of spider it is."

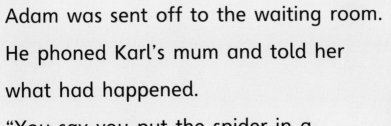

Adam was sent off to the waiting room. He phoned Karl's mum and told her what had happened.

"You say you put the spider in a lunchbox?" said Karl's mum. "There's a lunchbox here – but it's empty!"

"Empty?" said Adam. "Oh no!"

11

A bit later, a nurse came up to Adam.

"Your photo was brilliant," she said.

"The zoo knows what sort of spider it is.
Now we can give Karl the right medicine."

"Great!" said Adam. "I'll just get something
to eat, then I'll go and see him."

When he got to the café, Adam opened his bag. He did not see the beady eyes looking up at him. As Adam turned to pay, the spider crawled out of his bag. Out of the corner of his eye Adam saw something moving.

"No, it couldn't be!" he thought.

Adam went back to see Karl.

"He's going to be fine now," said the doctor. "Your photo saved his life."

"Guess what?" said Karl. "It turns out that the spider in the kitchen is one of the world's most deadly spiders. It's a Wandering Spider from South America. That bite could have killed me."

"It's a good thing you boys trapped it," said the doctor. "We can't have a deadly spider running around."

"But your mum has just told me that the spider isn't in the lunchbox," said Adam.

"What?" said Karl. "Where could it be?"

"Oh no," said Adam. "I've got a bad feeling about this."

"I think I might have seen the spider crawl out of my bag, when I was in the café," said Adam.

Adam and the doctor raced to the café. "I'm sure the spider will still be there," said Adam.
But it wasn't!

Quiz

Text Detective

- How did the mobile phone photo save Karl's life?
- How would you feel if you saw a big, black, hairy spider crawling up your arm?

Word Detective

- **Phonic Focus:** Unstressed vowels
  Page 11: Which letters represent the unstressed vowel in 'happened'? (en)
- Page 3: Find a word that means 'smiled'.
- Page 16: Why is there an exclamation mark right at the end of the story?

Super Speller

Read these words:

believe   only   happened

Now try to spell them!

HA! HA! HA!

Q What happens when a spider gets angry?

A He goes up the wall!

17

Find out about

• How people have survived terrible dangers

Tricky words

• lightning
• collarbone
• survived
• wearing
• canoe
• energy
• surfboard

Introduce these tricky words and help the reader when they come across them later!

Text starter

Would you chop off your leg to free yourself? Would you fight with a crocodile? What if a shark bit off your arm – would you paddle to the shore using just one arm? That's what people in this book did!

Do or Die

Crash!

The year is 1971.

Lightning hits the plane you are in.
The plane breaks up and you fall three
kilometres. You have broken your
collarbone and you can't see out of
one eye. What will you do?

1. Wait for help?

2. Set off to get help?

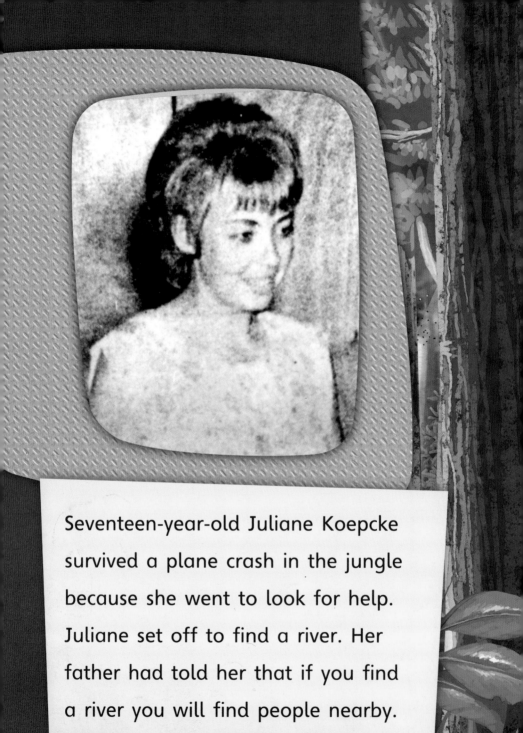

Seventeen-year-old Juliane Koepcke
survived a plane crash in the jungle
because she went to look for help.
Juliane set off to find a river. Her
father had told her that if you find
a river you will find people nearby.

Juliane walked for nine days.
She had no food. Leeches sucked her
blood and insects laid eggs under her skin.
Then the eggs began to hatch!
On day 10, Juliane came across a hut.
In the hut there was salt and petrol,
which she used to get the maggots
out of her skin.

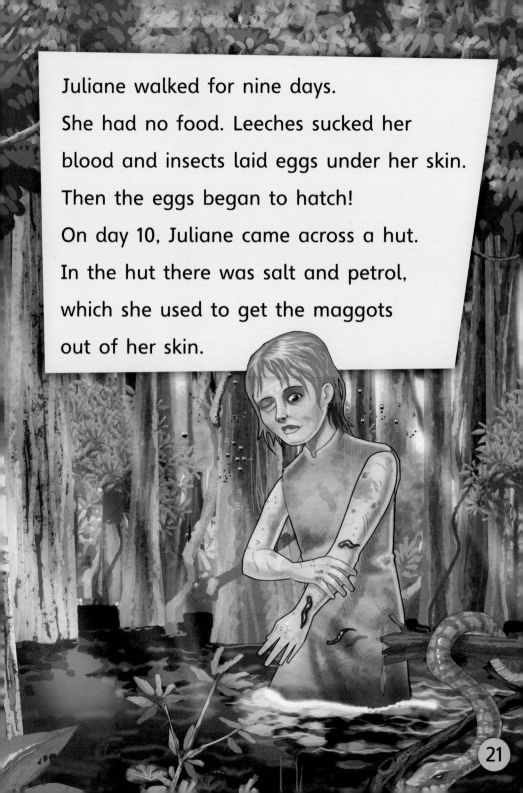

The next day, three local men arrived at the hut. The men led her to safety.

35 maggots came out of her arms.

There were 92 people on the plane. Fourteen people survived the crash, but they died before help arrived.
Juliane was the only one who survived.

Smash!

The year is 1993.

You are fishing in a river when rocks fall on you. You are trapped and your leg is smashed below the knee.

The sun is going down and a snow storm is starting. What will you do?

1. Wait until someone finds you?
2. Cut off your own leg?

Bill Jeracki was on a fishing trip when his leg was smashed. He hadn't told anyone where he was going and he was only wearing jeans and a T-shirt. The cold from the snow could kill him.

Should he lose his leg or his life?

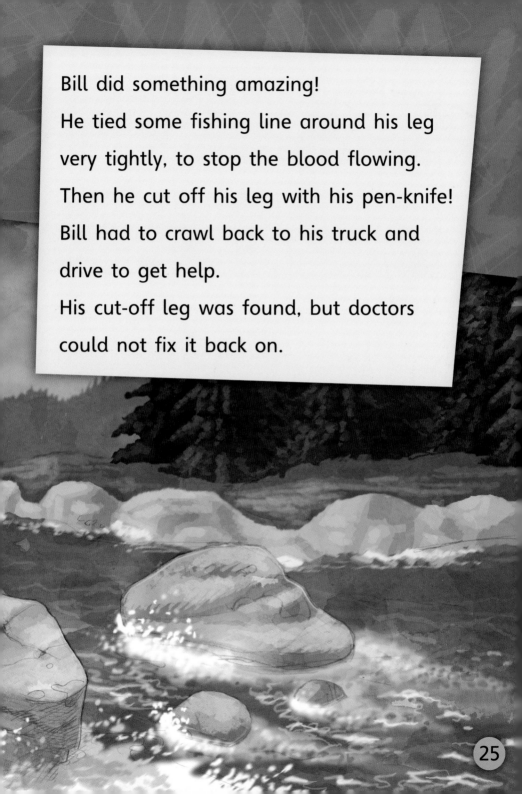

Bill did something amazing!
He tied some fishing line around his leg
very tightly, to stop the blood flowing.
Then he cut off his leg with his pen-knife!
Bill had to crawl back to his truck and
drive to get help.
His cut-off leg was found, but doctors
could not fix it back on.

Attack!

The year is 1995.

You are in a canoe on a river.

You see two big, yellow eyes.

It is a crocodile! You try to get out of the water, but the crocodile comes after you.

Snap! Jaws pull you into the water.

What will you do?

1. Give up?

2. Keep fighting?

Val Plumwood's canoe was attacked by a crocodile. When the crocodile dragged her under the water, she thought she would die.

But then the crocodile suddenly let go. Val swam up to the surface. She grabbed hold of a tree branch.

Could she get away?

No! The crocodile pulled Val back under the water, but it could not hold her down. Val got free again, but the crocodile pulled her back down for the third time. Val did not give up. She dug her fingers into the mud bank and dragged herself out of the river.

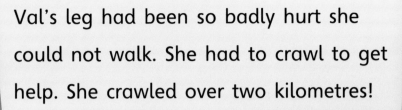

Val's leg had been so badly hurt she could not walk. She had to crawl to get help. She crawled over two kilometres!

Why had the crocodile let go of Val? Crocodiles only have the energy to fight for a short time. Val kept fighting and the crocodile gave up.

Snap!

The year is 2003.

You are on your surfboard.

A shark bites your left arm and tears it off.

You watch in shock as the water around

you turns bright red. What will you do?

1. Panic?

2. Stay cool?

This is what happened to thirteen-year-old Bethany Hamilton when she was surfing. Bethany stayed cool. With her right arm she paddled 400 metres to the shore.

Bethany lost her left arm, but she didn't let that stop her. As soon as she was well, she went back to surfing!

Quiz

Text Detective

- What have you learned about what to do if you are attacked by a crocodile?
- Do you think you would be brave in the face of terrible danger?

Word Detective

- Phonic Focus: Unstressed vowels
  Page 26: Which letters represent the unstressed vowel in 'water'? (er)
- Page 21: Find words that mean 'to break out of an egg'.
- Page 25: Why is there an exclamation mark at the end of the sentence about using the pen-knife?

Super Speller

Read these words:

water   wearing   watch

Now try to spell them!

HA! HA! HA!

Q What do you get when you cross a camera with a crocodile?

A A snap shot!